Breeze

The Ernest Sandeen Prize in Poetry

editor
John Matthias

2003, *Breeze,* John Latta

2001, *No Messages,* Robert Hahn

1999, *The Green Tuxedo,* Janet Holmes

1997, *True North,* Stephanie Strickland

Breeze

JOHN LATTA

UNIVERSITY OF NOTRE DAME PRESS
Notre Dame, Indiana

Notre Dame, Indiana 46556
http://www.undpress.nd.edu

Library of Congress Cataloging-in-Publication Data
Latta, John.
Breeze / John Latta.
p. cm. — (Ernest Sandeen prize in poetry ; 2003)
ISBN 0-268-02170-8
ISBN 978-0-268-02171-9 (pbk.)
I. Title. II. Series.

PS3562.A77 B74 2002
813'.54—dc21
2002012611

for

William Carl Latta

&

Harriet Mabon Latta

And then again the instant that I awoke methought I was a musical instrument—from which I heard a strain die out—a bugle—or a clarionet—or a flute—my body was the organ and channel of melody as a flute is of the music that is breathed through it. My flesh sounded & vibrated still to the strain—and my nerves were the chords of the lyre. I awoke therefore to an infinite regret—to find myself not the thoroughfare of glorious & world-stirring inspirations—but a scuttle full of dirt—such a thoroughfare only as the street & the kennel—where perchance the wind may sometimes draw forth a strain of music from a straw.

—*Henry David Thoreau*

Contents

Acknowledgments

Some of the poems in *Breeze* were first published in the following magazines:

American Letters & Commentary:	The Bones in El Bahnasa Blank, with Blandishments
Another Chicago Magazine:	*Morgenmusik*
Aufgabe:	Burning Issues
Barrow Street:	The Fort and Fortress of Our Certainty Depths and Approaches
The Beloit Poetry Journal:	Rock
Boog City:	Noting It Is Nothing
Chicago Review:	Reading Cicero's *De Oratore*
Exquisite Corpse:	Dusty Begonias The Upstart Petunia Herb and Violet The German Verb "To Twilight"
Fourteen Hills:	Wisdom Terrestrial and Nigh
The Germ:	Same Window A Template, Receding The Wag of the Inconsequent

The Gettysburg Review:	Night and Day in New York Beginning with a Line by Dino Campana For Boris Pasternak Perfect Sentences
Green Mountains Review:	Juvenilia Rue Taitbout
Gulf Coast:	Futility and Caprice in Yellow and Red
Hubbub:	A Singularity
ing:	Marketable
The Iowa Review:	Readerly Parisian Miniatures
Lingo:	In the Margins of a Book by Heidegger
Mike & Dale's Younger Poets:	The Weather
Notre Dame Review:	The Limits of Language Look A Jack Spicer Notebook At Nags Head Glib Dirty Weather Order and Accident
No Røses Review:	Earnest Bookish, Clowning
The Paris Review:	*Elogio di* Frank O'Hara
Phoebe:	*Mon nom est personne*
Poetry International:	A Notebook of First Permission

Ribot:	Exclusive
Seneca Review:	Chants of a Myrmidon *Explication de texte* Testimony, Eradicable
Skanky Possum:	Expiring at the Edge of the Old Empire
Sulfur:	To Robert Duncan
Sycamore Review:	Poem Like a Tree or a Bus
Verse:	North Carolina Notebook
Willow Springs:	John Latta, in a Copybook Garden Variety Stories

My thanks to all the editors for their interest and good work. Thanks also to the National Endowment for the Arts for a grant that helped provide the time needed to prepare the manuscript of *Breeze* for publication.

NATIONAL
ENDOWMENT
FOR THE ARTS

Breeze

In the Margins of a Book by Heidegger

Daily chores impinge, poking
Little subsets of clarity into the unutterable
Stink of thinking just as a philodendron,
Flexing, furls its tame blue fingers around a newel post
Or a doorjamb and is given to support and temper the wild both.
And somewhere a man keeps glancing at a watch, angry
With an identifiable lateness ticked off
In minutes so that he misses the minute
Particulars of a mockingbird's singular loud triads.

He would rather not be out this morning
Waiting for the bus that'll transport
Him, hatted and usual, to the job he hates.
The French triumvirate of *métro, boulot, dodo*
Breaks like a succession of tiny suns rising
Over a glorious day already too full of nouns, too full
Of nouns that work to congeal the beckoning stillness
That, once in motion, moves him into enchantment
And endless conversation: that ongoing effortless grant

To return to whatever is arriving.

Noise

Off in the distance, the sound of
A truck backing up to unload a cargo
Of roofing material, as if distance were a container,

As if absence kept its pennies in its fist.
That's one way. Another is noise
That jitters the portico, slams

Doors to mark a threshold, to incinerate
A context where meaning camps, direct
Fiduciary mayhem spending its own

Against the bank, a tension
Snapping syntactical guy wires, obliterative,
Sizzling, the long days of clot and release,

The prim mercy of the thank-yous
Coming out of mouths, tiny curtains of night
And a grackle black and inescapable as a plinth.

Like play money, noise
Does not exist in itself, it comes into being
Only in deference to a whole chorus of expenditures

And debts
And adumbrates by the gentlest mockery
A system otherwise inestimably lit.

Black pennies in the hand of whosoever is
Doing the daily handouts.
We plunk our tokens down, buying back

The world in pieces whilst
Noise comes a-
Cropper, does its aw-

Shucks turnabout just
To make music
Listen.

Morgenmusik

A syllabary of noise tending to white:
Behemoth gleeps and susurrus, the French
Word for key. Out of the din a tonality
Emerges, a series of probabilities we stake
High stakes to, betting that tempo itself
Points to recognition. Or we fall back to narrative:
A Polish girl with a straight smile
Gone nasty with drink. First she calls the taxi
Driver a dirty Arab, second she loses her sandals
In the Parc de Vincennes, third she . . .
The sequence carries an emotional charge, something
We manipulate, divvying up events
As prior to a number of possible outcomes
And pointing to one in particular, a result
That makes necessary and defines the addends
That make it up. Frankly, mornings
I'd rather approach such a threshold
In oscillatory blink and bemusement, my vibrato
Declaring a dynamism I like to think of
As Einsteinian, voice expelling
A roll of units discrete and continuous as hubbub's
Own sown hubbub is, a business hard enough
To foster without exemplum and dash.
So a senator parks a Toyota under the dais, awestruck
By the pinch and release of the bunting's blue . . .
So two toy iotas of mischief invade
The blue eyes of an actress who is trying
To work up a sob, adding poignant bits
Of information briefly to the scene just before
The houselights come up and everything again goes white.

The Morning News

Brings reports beyond ken, the shrugs
Of defiant aggressors, a Florida panhandler's heroics
In a weather of black twisters, the slaughter

And sprawl of the usual
Ragged bodies in African dust.
Dents in the helmet the blue-green globe's

Been wearing now for centuries.
A tight-fitting thing, with a chin-strap
Pulling its jaw up and shut, forcing the grimly emergent

Howl back down, unspeakable, rote.
What complaints you shout out carry no weight,
Torn away by casual winds too full of agony

To notice or stop.
Words you set such store by, hoarding
A whole gamut of innuendo and minutiae

In that finite system of marks struck so cleanly black
On cream-colored rag paper, those words run
A sad gauntlet between big art and a life

That cannot empty itself of restlessness.
It thumps sudden and furious in its sleep like a dog.
And today the stores are full of bargains

On containers for rage, amazing
Little *weltanschauung*-ready collections of stories,
So affably hurting, so love-prompted and other.

There's a little history you know something about, yes,
And who needs it? The words
Line up so gracefully, sincere

Cogs in the dirty clockwork machinery.
To keep the whole thing running,
To keep the world beyond ken

Going and going and going
Like a little miniature toy
Inside the perfect helmet of your head.

Chants of a Myrmidon

Unscrupulous attention to detail is necessary:
The blue box of the television slanting out its containment
Of nebulous light

Draws a line that cuts off the viewer's ankle, severs a notorious
    tendon.
The upcoming war is the main event and the tendency is
To notice that and leave off any pining

For the reckless sundry energies elsewhere
Under no command.
A dog's paw thumps the rug

Weaving the Morse code of a hunt
Into the sounds of gunfire and sirens out the open window.
And a spoon lying tangent to a coffee cup

Is pulling down pieces of a broken-up radio signal,
    rebroadcasting
The stray vibrato notes of a 1939 Texaco *Norma*
With an unforgettable Italian in the title role.

I cannot get today the usual behoovings of my cry
Not to contain any brook
I brook no quarrel with . . .

It is going along singing mightily of the lesser slumbers, what
Consciousness wakes up in attending to its own
Wake

As it pulses ahead or rips like a motorboat
At full throttle, too much horsepower for any little stream.
And my waves slog through

Primordial black mud, water-
Log the dwarf iris, the arrowhead, the turtle
Sunning itself and whose subsequent mad scramble

Draws the attention of the least flycatcher stuck
To the overhanging willow limb, upright as an incisor.
I am not and I admit it

Really getting this movie—it's the one with the forgettable
    Achilles
Played by that smooth talker with the dimple.
It's all going over my head, up

Into the draperies that block any light coming through
The window out of which I can see anything
But what I do not choose to.

Same Window

This has to do with sitting where I sit most days
Gazing out. I am not exactly waiting, though I am
Attentive to the liminal drifting vociferousness

Of hesitance and all its furtive charms—
That's how I like to put it.
I become aware of a low barely perceptible hum,

Like an artillery barrage, as if a TV set
Tuned to a documentary about Dien Bien Phu
Were lodged in a giant bale of cotton

Suspended by cable and crane over the hold
Of a freighter, stopped mid-
Air by off-

Loading longshoremen stopped for a lunch break.
They untwist thermos caps, unwrap thick sandwiches, talk
Ordinary sports and unionization, oblivious

To the sniping and ricochet and moan of
A battle muffled by batting.
What is present is not the war itself.

Canned and adulterated, its humanizing solace is this one
Of sheer receptivity, like that day
Hiking the blue Virginia ridges, blue

And quelled by the interstellar world,
That day when the metal in my teeth began to broadcast
Human voices,

A press conference slicing the air-
Waves all the way out of Topeka.
That was years ago, and the voices—you swore one was
    Dean Rusk,

One Jimmy Hoffa.
A towheaded boy goes by the same window now,
Bat on shoulder, mitt

Hanging like a small glazed ham off a belt.
He's got an air of nothing doing,
And doing nothing is plenty enough for you.

Testimony, Eradicable

Nary a cloud and I
At my usual post, a drifting boundary marker, sentient
Pinpoint needling the gauzy interstices,
Trying to get a purchase in a fabric too thin to hold.

Or the cloth is good, a tapestry wove of bird, grass, mountain.
The implacable green shiny leaves of the maple, lordly
Constituent of the legislature of now and I am
Witness sewn in to the all.

I am the dropped stitch, present
By absence, a flaw in the nothingness
Where nothingness lacks nothing.
I am the hack behoover, nudging

Voicelessness up against raw science, or raw silence.
This is a little difficult to depict, the explanatory
Ways stand akimbo, impatiently thumping one foot or the other,
Thinking time is running out. It is.

The final billions of particles, its last random leavings,
Course through the narrows, velocitizing the quick.
So I lob the moon up over the horizon
Where big as a platter it races away

Diminishing to dinnerplate, saucer, dotty
Aunt Ruth's bone china coaster.
To say I am dust, unlegislated and traveling,
To say I see my energies in the miniature currents and vortices

Of a barnacle pumping tidewater
Through its fibrillating hairlike whatevers,
To admit the gone spectaculars of my desire are now
Clotting the manure factories of a bacterial city

Caked to the underside of a horse's hoof—
Is to relent to a contagion like no other, or like the one
That makes me sandwich words amongst the layers
Of pigweed and grass clippings in a compost

Heap like no other, ready for the world
With its final billions of threads to announce itself
Wearing nothing, no garment like this that
Nary a cloud'd wear.

Beginning with a Line by Dino Campana

Like a cloud coming to a dead stop
In uproarious sky, my recklessness
Pauses to announce its earnest, a solitary thing

Ready to inveigle the big
Dispersal or make corporeal the tactile
Whims of the blue bump and rub of air against air.

Or I cannot stop the sleepy orbit.

I am a cloud stuck into the trousers'
Pocket of the world's otherworldly doings, doing
What it does like a little noun

Tagging along behind a big verb.
And I am ever near
To the saying of what is unsayable, an honest-to-God
Asymptote nearing the imaginary

Coordinate of the x-axis,
Laying the trace of my approach down
Like a vapor trail, its invisible pinpoint
Widening to blot the whole
Dear blue sky.

What matters is not matter, is not
How you undertook to call out to the clouds
Who were leaving, "Hey, wait up, guys!"
And immediately thought better of it, rather

Enjoying the sour odor of abandonment.
It gives you something to palm in moments of skittish bravado.
Or palm off. A mystery of who you were in the weather
Of those days. No more. And no more elegies.

No more lines about the cupric glint of tiny Greek flowers.
No more lines about the geometries of loss and desire.
Put a hand in your pocket and fish out some pennies.
What good are pennies to a cloud?

Elogio di *Frank O'Hara*

Now that I am up here in the sky I can see
The *mare di San Tommaso* is a puddle of ink,
A hierarchy of imperial blue tints, tempting
The way order often is. No stranger's foot
Weighs on my heart and the earth today, howsoever
Cloud-begrudged and fickle, is turning
Itself "to" the unbudging sun though we're slow
To end our geocentric habits of three meddlesome centuries
Of science leading us by the dirty hand and do not desist
In saying the sun "rises," inexpert with the language
That exists merely to placate our sensibilities,
Troubled by the evacuations of art, how it leaves
Adamant puddles in the landscape that go to work
On the imaginations of stragglers like you and me.
You got through it all through pure charm,
Like a little grinning quark, knowing bravado
To be as specious as any other absolute, dashing
Naked into the night-stormy ocean, the only man awake
On earth and nobody left up to play with.
If we make our own suspicious amusements up and leave
Too many things undone it's because life is a work-
In-progress like any work is, always open and remaining so.
So it transpires that we must needs fill somebody's shoes
With feet of clay, feet broken off a statue
We've been lugging around on our shoulders
For a number of decades now not knowing
Exactly where to put it, in the kitchen or out
In the dreary afternoons of Vaughan Williams and rain
And a caravansary of words all leaking largesse, ambassadors
Of a perception that arrives in pieces, the way
A walk up along the ridge above Fiesole

Makes the path drop away, invisible
As the angels, the spectators, the sky-
Borne millions though we see now how the path continues
As descent and know it and we and they and you are there.

Juvenilia

All of it is, and unfinished is . . .
That man in the shorts and baseball
Cap sure's got a funny way of walking, as if

Every step is the partial retrieval of a memory
Of some previous step
He longs to take. The present is like that.

Inadequate recalled designs on the upcoming moment
When the bird caught in the ribcage
You made to hold only a heart

Opens the acute dark parallelogram of its mouth
And pours forth a reckless song, a wandering
Curlicue of omission made desire, mission

Made grace, when there's nothing to do
Except accept, expert as you are at excerpting the whole
From any available part.

Or say it differently. Say an arm reaches down
To pluck you off your porch and transport you swaying
Like a pendulum's bob

Up into the timepiece's perpetual pert music, smooth
Wheels spinning in oily light, and in the midst
Gears like teeth biting out an irregular backbeat, whatever

Makes the hands sweep evenly forward only to return.
You too would put your own hands to your own face like
    a clock.
You too would note the distance between

The future and how you remember it and recall
Recalling that moment of crying
At the moment you will burst into tears.

The Weather

Just no letup to it.
At nine-twenty of a Tuesday, mulling over events of a decade lost
To a succession of tiny skirmishes

With despair and random acts of pointless retrieval like the night
You slept in the courtyard shrubbery of
A primary school in Strasbourg, woke

To a half-circle of tykes in short pants beaming like seraphs, like
    sinecures, like work-
Horses, all traversing the dim arc of seeing
Like figures of the zodiac—water carrier,

Ram, the scales, the twins, representations of things that become
    things
Only through the adamant name-
Calling that tortures our dream

Of a world of pure objects . . .
One tyke tosses a soccer ball that bounces off your word-
Foolish round head and the others applaud noiselessly, a sign

That the common exigencies of language
Lapse, and thankfully, pinned down as you are by peculiar inner
    weathers,
The late tally of several Yugoslavian beers

Drunk grim as if in a quandary
Or in a Quonset hut deep in post-Kansan light . . .
Planning to go to Oz, planning to retrieve Dorothy

Who slips between the numbers
Into the sixes and sevens of your own indifference . . .
Blame the weather. Blame the critical mass of whim, a boat-

Load of bad books, words
Going down with the boat that provides its own ballast
    as ballast
And never doubt the sanity of anything so round as a round-
    about head

Water runs off and raindrops
Through with being
Raindrops pool in a spreading pocket of sun.

For Boris Pasternak

Two hens, bobbing to drink, disturb
The perfect landscape that lies in a puddle
In a barnyard flatly illustrated

As if a page in a picture book
Carried by a boy in stiff trousers
Had come loose and slipped out, becoming

Memory by simple dint of disappearing so.
He walks and hums a little melody of the great life to come.
He is going to a stark and brutal precipice to shout

Against the indifference of the sea, he is going
To the unobtrusive market town of S——— to devote himself
To the piano or to the blistering sigh

Inserted like a knife into tawdry dull conversations
Of red-faced commissars, earnest bureaucrats
Who line pockets with tobacco curls, or lint.

He is the inventor of a look
That makes cutlery poised on the fingers of ladies
Tip ringingly to china, makes teacups topple against the samovar.

That boy . . . and people shake great, knowing heads.
That boy loves the slim white birches that edge the property—
How they shine like straw blades in a dark tangle of hair!—

The whole muss and lambency of the observable world.
That boy knows those trees as sisters
To a life pulled down like a book

Read once for the sleepy pleasure of it all, once
For the lethal certainty of knowing all the details,
Once for the fine ache of knowing knowing perishes. . . .

The Limits of Language

Days like today, the intermittent rain
Drumming its particular rain-
Carnival rhythms off the eaves, its dense patter

Of faulty vocables, its unspeakable overlaps of
Noise, *thrup-thrup, thrup-thrup,*
With a skirling addition, a high

Persistent keening, a *thrip-thrip,* randoming
The backbeat, overburdening
The interstices: these days language is no good for.

If we itch to make mention of the rain
And its hugger-mugger way of talking,
We need—in all our endless primal itchiness—

To offer ourselves without intention,
Without words,
To other transports elsewhere—*intermezzo,*

Tintoretto, harlequinade, minuet—
Any smeary coincidence the world can muster.
Somewhere someone says:

"We cannot talk in simultaneous bunches of names."
Exactly. Talking we atomize the world
To rearrange it, to string

Strings of whatever few particulars can be strung,
Forgetting, like any child
Content with bead-stringing, how

The necklace only calls attention to the whole
Cloth of the chemise, how
It is not the essential wearable itself.

So we stop talking
Just as the rain,
In a lengthy diminuendo, thins itself to a temporary halt.

Though we hardly notice it:
Our feet, unbeknownst to our feet, move
Now in easy reiteration,

Now in cumbersome jest, speaking
The gone rain's story, happy
Geniuses of the story of the gone rain.

Freud says somewhere that every *move* is a *gesture,* meaning
We carry something along with us,
Some extraordinary kind of freight

Filling up our little carts,
The freight of a cart of raindrops,
The freight of a caboose of *rainingness* itself,

All hodge-podge and overlay, freight
We dearly long to discharge . . .
And if I pull my earlobe in a distant quiet way,

Will the whole load of rainy expressiveness get dumped, or
Shunted down a spur track, one
Just there for the unloading? Not exactly.

The instrumentality of the tug becomes its own end—and here
I remain, an upright animal
Toying with an appendage, standing

Akimbo in a kind of becoming perplexity
Like a painter whose smock is dotted and re-
Dotted to a pleasing *drench*

By the spritzing accident of the unbecoming rain.
There's a story I am longing to tell about the limits of language,
An untellable story.

I knew a man who, weary
Of the linear, the discrete, the successive
Order of words, wrote

What he called *A Novel on the Head of a Pin.*
He read some of it to me one day, a soothing babble.
He claimed it was about "everything, everything simultaneously,

All words, all letters in a rush, a swirl, a concentrate."
He showed me a copy. It looked like this: •
What I want to say is this:

This rain, letting up now, still
Capable of a squall, a blurry contingency overloading
The whole wet scene, this rain is more than language can bear.

Blank, with Blandishments

Something momentous and occasional
Like a sale in a French hardware store
Is about to reveal itself through the pettifoggery

Of itself, though, inevitably,
Interruptions'll hoosegow the business
Just to make it richer. Poor reader.

Just a telephone call away.
I am out here in the peripheries of the gorgeous
Word and there you are stuck

Centre ville where the tourist
Office stands empty though chock-
Full of brochures, maps and whatnot, all

Perfectly arranged by sites historical and near, marvelously
Illustrated, and set mostly in Garamond,
A roman-letter type first cut in the early 16th c.

And notable for its refusal to imitate handwriting.
It did become a standard, legible, clean, aligned
Often with "grace." I do so mind the fact

That you cannot be here with me, don't
Think I don't. It's what my peevishness is
All about, that and the inexpressible need I have

To pester the superfluous
In a terrible reaching after the absolute.
That same old same old. Thank God

The telephone is ringing now.
I know someone will get it, someone "unlocatable" perhaps,
Though reliable as a machine

Picking up by the fourth ring
To announce calmly in a voice not unlike your own
That nobody's home right now.

It lets you know somehow
That home is here, reader,
Even if vacant, even if unreached.

Smoke

Rhythm, unavoidable, makes a ratio—
That's the long and short of it.

Pulses, jamming, pick the continuous indifference of the world
  apart,
Lay the yaw and pitch of it down at our feet, a thing

We can't ever get close to due to the wordy undertow, more
  things.
Example: what's drawn howling out of the ample,

A fleet throbbing particular standing in for the quavery whole.
It offers only an emotional currency, one

Indispensable, the way a Liberty silver dollar today
Fits no vending slot, no machine.

Here's what I'm talking "about."
I use the term loosely, finessing the structure itself

By the crude means of its absence, the way
An artist often works up an intricate crosshatching

Around the round newel post.
Not so much to define it as to suggest its presence

By making a grid of attention surround that place
Where definition longs one day to stand.

He lets repetition and variation do the work,
Tiny slant lines whose overlaps hint of depth and a nostalgia

For certitude and its irrecoverable anxieties.
Done, he erases the whole mess and titles it *Smoke*

And hangs it over the fireplace
In front of which you are now reading this

Or feeding it piece by piece into ordinary vague flames,
Noting the only thing in the world that will not burn is smoke.

Dirty Weather

The white fluff off the cottonwoods bordering the park
Marks the exact number of little local breezes
Out in the air today. Here on the porch I am stationary, just
A camera on a tripod, trying to figure out a link
Between *destiny* and *density* and thinking about a friend
Who's become a Pinkerton Agency man in Asia.

He's a talker, entirely "talk-oriented" as one says, a funny way to
put it,
Seeing as I can't say I've heard much of him in a tortoise's life-
Span of years. How do the English call it? A spanner? What
I call a wrench and now need to undo the one large nut
That keeps my ass bolted down to the seat of my chair,
A folding metal model, rather like the aforementioned tripod.

Am I getting feedback? The vernacular always makes it appear so.
I remember when movies were mostly clever talk, rapid
Repartee and rejoinder. The set just sat there
Or a door made out of canvas moved occasionally
Ever so slightly, the result of a breeze. Weather-
Making machines were all the rage—the rain-

Stung or wind-lashed moor available at a nod.
I find it curiously sad that my friend the talker is a Pinkerton man.
It's as if he were now in a movie, something with Elisha
Cook as the oyster-eyed thug who steps out into the typhoon, out
Around the potted palm outside the Hotel Destiny
And into the dirty weather just in time to get his.

Somebody's turned off the wind-machine now and the cottonwood
fluff
Is settling down, gathering its own density.
I could shoot the talker's adventures in Gstaad next—
The divorcee's champion dog, the revolver in the bathtub, the
dropped ski-
Lodge book of matches . . . I could put it all in in one single take
And it would take a talking detective to figure out what I'm
talking about.

A Singularity

No occasion beyond the smudge of writing,
The event itself
Enacting a spate of units, measure
Forcing the hand.

A crow slices the morning airs
With hoarse triplets, carves
A niche in the understory of available noise.
It's up in the Norway spruce, sentinel

To the tiniest acts of its own activity.
The immediate vicinity is rife
With concomitant world-
Making, mostly unseen:

A greenish grasshopper is stepping off
Grasshopper-sized steps
To find the fulcrum
Of the lever of grass it is climbing.

Ridiculous discourse. Logic colonizes
An interior susceptible to itself, one
Too malleable, too plastic
To break by heaving.

We dabble in drugs that do nothing, and music,
And note the informing brash structures
That, paramecia-like, engulf
Our breakages, whole, digestible, apace.

Rife is the music—*sinecure, tiny palace, a boy named Stumpy*—
Rife the systematic embodiments of it
In the whole sorry sprawl,
The elsewhere

Where the world is not.
The heave is the word breaking into use—mouth-
Ruptures opening up the bee hum of totality
Into distinct raptures, physical, strewn and any

Walk in the yard is forever and again
Going simply to be
The walk in the yard,
Irrepeatable, blessèd, new.

Parisian Miniatures

Ambulatory doubt, you
Step into radiance only because whose.

*

An occasion for thinking about the little executions of dusk,
    following
The summer's bigger.

*

You, trumpet of ennui in honey-
Yellow Hopper light aslant as an open door.

*

The kind of rumpled look all the post office clerks acknowledge,
With quick additions.

*

Preliminary to delineating,
Something major like a foot in a jackboot.

*

Writing under the imprimatur of the private culpability of.

*

Undeliverable, like that swastika
Appended to a postcard to Graham, unthinkingly.

*

Of the maestro, no word, so you look at a program about bird
dogs
In Normandy, and such gear.

*

The Austrian boy translating a play by Sacher-Masoch keeps
ordering stingers.

*

Transistor radio underneath a pillow and here comes the BBC—
bong, bong, bong.

*

Every cahoots you get yourself into turns out to warrant
Some kind of impossibly wordy certificate.

*

Around the fountain's periphery carp roll like oranges,
Like warnings, like signs.

*

A girl in Codec is selling slices of blood oranges, lithe
Uninhabitable prize like a lighthouse.

*

Understudy to an actor who threw a voice like a grappling hook
Up six stories of nineteenth-century wall.

*

Alarming the way a clock bequeaths the day with slippage, brash
As a gangster, on the lam.

*

Two episodes having to do with a sleeping bag
Lined with illustrations of duck hunters in red plaid caps.

*

So what if you walk all the streets "in a doozy of a wine-blunt
    analphabetic fog"?

*

You, cabinet of curiosities—Street of the Woman without a Head,
Street of the Man Who Waves and Waves.

*

City of grit caught in the eyelid's watery, too distant horizon.

Rue Taitbout

Everything's about duration, like
The question invariably put first, a kind
Of poultice, a bandage to soak up our youth—

How long you been traveling?—though, in truth, we aren't.
Or I am, and you not. Traveling as a wound travels,
Or a mollusk or a scab: stuck

To an idea of something akin to motion,
Motionless, feeding. You are translating uncertainty
Into a love affair with a place

In that endearing and innocent more-French-than-the-French way.
Or you reject that. Or I do. There are a number of possibilities,
All blind to the pretenses of narrative,

As narrative itself is blind and so possible.
You go off to the Schwarzwald, or to Norway and its fjords
And send back enigmatic postcards

About dropping acid near Ballon d'Alsace—
"I stand here like a semaphorist
Smack dab atop a pine-circled mountain and see

All the trees as one cubist tree, all
Overlay and disarray and simultaneity."
Or I return to the room, to the one window

Overlooking the one tree, a horse
Chestnut, courtyard straggler or emissary to some country
I do not know.

I pin a newspaper to the dormer-
Slant wall and draw a large rhinoceros.
I keep the rents

In the future pinned together, mending
My loneliness with flimsy blue *aerogrammes* I cover
With words that seem amiable enough

To be able to become whatever things they refer to—
And I don't ever consider the audacity
Of one world outside becoming another one *in.*

Sad mottled city
Pigeons peck holes in the shiny tops of the yoghurt containers
I leave on the window's ledge.

The slanting sun turns
The clay chimneys to fiery copper, or sienna,
Colors I can reach with the paintbrush I have ready.

The world is moving on—traveling—
In a hundred directions *out*
Like the smithereens aftermath of an *attentat,* all

Fragment and trajectory while our long-winded lines
Of distress and conjecture provide no adequate
Order, just a salve, endurable, endured.

Noting It Is Nothing

Under weather imitant of that
Of a French colonial outpost, fan-
Stir, drench and general allover irritability,

I do not desire any *beignets* today, howsoever
Light, howsoever pecky with crumbs of white sugar.
I do not want want to determine need, shuttering

Out the lithe jabber of the fungi sellers,
Purveyors of lemongrass and innumerable varieties of curry, whole
Conversations of spice, counterthrust and feint,

O the rhythmic savory imbroglios of a scorching mouthful . . .
There's a word for what I am experiencing today,
Though that word only draws an arc in haze,

An incomplete circle, and requires more words
Just as a spur track that leads one into a still and tender landscape
Overhung with bougainvillea does so only by dint of veering

Off the main line, the one that goes north
To assume contours of land it knows is bare scrim
And retort to its careful threading.

It's like this: the stationmaster's little girl
Is making soap bubbles, floating round mirrors, replicas
Of what desire is

With its ongoing need to dress up the here and now—
The sleepy rickshaw driver on the platform, slumping
Against red brick, batting away a curious kitten,

Et cetera—and so render its grace in a tumble of vocabulary.
I want only to undress this moment of knowing, forgetting
Speech in a human blaze unadulterated and skeletal

As the bubble's shiny continents
Go skinny as lattice-
Work and break.

Futility and Caprice in Yellow and Red

Six yellow tulips and two red, wild.
The word *Euclidean* insinuates its short diminuendo
Into the scene, and *cinnabar.*

What begins in noticing, in the immediate noose
Of the *here,* stumbles up against umpteen centuries of
Canned distinctions and a music

Slopping side to side like milk in a pail.
That's not too precise. What I mean is a man
Who sits looking out over a disused field

Where the ruins of a cabin poke up through green
Timothy and yarrow and the tiniest smudge
Of a garden plot

Plots a history, prefigures a life
Of small bent figures trudging out, black
Cutouts against the yellow sun,

Laboring to feed livestock with peculiar names—
Biltmore, Adeline, Zephyr—
Or hoeing white cabbages in the white

Light of the moon.
Maybe a wife tends beds of color, swaying
Geometries cut to endorse

Any passing, the invalid daughter
Sarah gone to typhoid.
Or maybe not.

There's a certain futility to landscape's
Desire to deny whatever alters it, the way a sentence
Like *There's a perfect plate, a World's*

Fair commemorative edition,
Lying in blackberry brambles
Down by the dump is a mere collection of nouns, inert

Begrudging murderesses of the tempestuous
Array, the antic verity that's not too precise.
Come here. Look for yourself.

At Nags Head

We lope single file down the Beach Road,
Counting the different ways of spelling
Omelette at the earlybird breakfast joints.

And every day the brown pelicans go by, singly
Skimming the wave-troughs south or
North in squads of five or

Six arrowing over the dunes.
What kind of behavior is that? I like the way
That pelican's little head looks

Like a cue ball in the sun.
Doodlebugs hiding in tiny craters below the deck
Spit back geysers of sand

If we tickle the peripheries with something,
Timothy grass or twig. I read Fenollosa
Who says there is no grammar in nature, no noun.

He is trying to posit Chinese as a language
Where being is never simply being: it is always *doing*,
All process and motion unstilled by mere sign.

I admit it: I am restless as a Chinaman today.
On the beach we walk the foam-edge, there
Where the ocean hikes up its lace skirt.

We find a square ray, a stiff brown parallelogram
With a tail, desiccated, rubbery. What mishap
Of stranding, what single midnight's blue

Wave's unwitnessed glorious push
Left it there like a geometric marker, a clue
To the ancient verb of the sea?

I am restless. Here. It is still May.
The wind keeps blowing. Deep in the primordial
Night we exchange light shivery dream-doings—

Of leaving, of being left. You curl like a cloud
Around me and we sleep and wake
To a morning of hundreds of clouds.

North Carolina Notebook

The road to the pier collapses under the slow brunt of relict dune
Deposits, blown.

*

The mystery of the line of cormorants perch'd on pilings, black
Wings shrug'd out, still:

One hour's tenuous purchase on the day, unspent.

*

Rapturous bob and drill of sanderlings and turnstones,
Ruddy, individual, schooling:

The gem-stuck skirt of ocean.

*

Prickly pear and sheep sorrel snarling up traffic in the lower
Kingdoms of dune grass.

*

Sky gone to brooding, particle-heavy, at dusk, knits itself to
wooly acres of spume.

*

A lone laughing gull, black head turning like a knob,
Beats mercy back by crying

Mercy,
            mercy

Up through the slipstream of wind trying to go around wind.

*

Dwarf pines dotting the sinkholes. Hummocky nether regions.

*

Lumps of human color, salt-stung, hallooing without sound.
Dashing pitiably at waves,
                                        in waves.

Garden Variety Stories

I championed narrative for a number of sluggish years, then decided against its way of spotlighting the social when my habits became increasingly those of a hermit-saint, puttering about in downpours tending my sensational potatoes.

So a story begins, or might, with a voice swooping down out of the logical north to ransack your monastic neural fortress, heaping with barbaric glee cadences unidentifiable and plotted on what you have grown to consider *your own little patch of earth.* You have never charted it very carefully over the years, never made diagrams of the rotations of radishes and peas, or any of the more unusual crops you have sometimes strewn about in your laughably impertinent manner.

Your interest is just not in the jut of the jaw of the man who is always tightening a bolt on a weed whacker, or in the way that man's tongue always finds itself stuck half out, clamped between teeth like a stogie whenever he's got a chore to do. Your way is not to view the vegetable kingdom as a temporary transcendent hollow, or as a way of leaving this world with its rainy interruptions aside *en route* to the sober triumphs of the beyond. Your way is to participate in the ongoing loud transformation, and if hailstones
the size of small cabbages
hurtle out of the changeable sky
one day wiping out the cabbages
you were not put on this earth just to grow, remember that
loss is its own indemnity, and this
story, like light, is not anything
you'll ever be able to hold in your hands.

Readerly

I read "Grammatically realized meaning is a postponed
reward . . ."
And think how rewarding a scoop or even larger helping of
vanilla
Ice cream can be after the loud and long rain delays and
postponements of a broadcast
Double-header, Sunday afternoon, a little lazy, the tiny rug of
grass, all dew-

Besmirch and ringlet, cut in a few idle minutes this morning, cut
By starting at one corner (call it *A*) of the rectangle and moving
to the one adjacent (*B*)
And pivoting the roaring mower ninety degrees
To proceed to corners *C* and *D* with the practiced indifferent
maneuvers of a man

Who knows the book he is reading begins on page one and
proceeds
Step by pleasant step through a tangle of signifiers, each
Shorn by the blades of vision and usual procedure, the clippings
collected in the grass-
Stained bag of ratiocination (a reassurance), though not
*reason*ably sorted

Are they, but kept unkempt just as he keeps to a comfortable
stride
Marking a pattern, a ziggurat in the yard, cornering
Well, making boxes within boxes in order to finish before the
game starts
Because the game offers its own rewards, like a pitcher who
discusses *with* the baseball

The baseball's incipient trajectory, where it should arrive
Being where it desires arriving,
Though in practice (that is, in the real game
Being played out there now on the rain-soaked diamond) it

(The baseball) will always miss by a few gaping inches, that gap
Being where the batter swings and misses with a sheer
    undifferentiated
Discharge of energy (accompanied by a grunt) just north of
Intention, just south of where the ball *thwacks* the mitt

Of the hunkering untalkative catcher who knows nothing
    anymore of desire now
Because that strikeout (a kind of erasure) ends the game
And he is easeful in loping to the dugout, to the showers, thinking
How terrific a scoop of ice cream is, or how a book

A woman—a red-haired fan in short shorts and halter top—
    had one day
Read to him seemed then like everything in the world, just as she
    did,
And later like only what (and not, he thinks, much it was) had
    been ". . . attained
By arrival at the end of a horizontal, linearized sequence of words."

Reading Cicero's De Oratore

I

The edge of the text is where we sample the remarkable, as if gist were a kind of outward drift, pith a sponginess only substituting for the absent center.

Ezra Pound, whom we forgive, knew this. He "tried to write Paradise" and found only wind—what goes and goes, ruffling the borders, the hedgerows,

tossing, like scrap paper, a flock of juncos (and the odd sparrow) into itself. Letting the wind speak *is* Paradise, that thing known only by its *passing*

through, its *going elsewhere,* a shiftless continuum moving ever generously over unbordered mountain and forest and town. Cicero wasn't the first man to inhabit one of those towns, though

town life agreed with a need to mark boundaries, to dispel the wild filigree of the countryside, that tangle, what he called "the rabble of rusticity," ever-

encroaching, unknowledgeable, uninstructed. He was the first man to use the word "urbanity" and mean not just "citified" but "refined

by means of proper confinement." For without the boundaries of knowledge, Cicero thought, discourse is only "an empty and ridiculous swirl of verbiage"—

that "empty" recalling the sweet captivating roominess, what lies around the rustic's camp, that "swirl of verbiage" announcing the dangerous thicket within.

II

I love the story of Themistocles, the Athenian endowed with an unstoppable memory, a monstrous city of memory, all of whose inhabitants, having one day entered its prodigious gates,

were bound to remain, tearing about in toil and truckle, as if in a wilderness, wolf-haunted, unrent and rude. And I love how a man, a quack (he pulled a gilt cart, he did a little show)

"offered to impart to the Athenian the science of mnemonics, then being introduced for the first time." And Themistocles refused, seeking "the greater kindness"—forgetfulness.

Behind the story, of course, is a fear of disorder, a fear of a seamless world. A fear of going where the wind, ever-speaking, goes.

I remember a poet one day saying with only a trace of North Carolina raillery, with pale blinking innocence undone by a flicker of sass, not unlike a boy

striking out for an excursion in the woods: "I think a poet ought to keep himself just a little stupid." Pure Cicero, really. For what is knowledge but a means of leaving some things out,

a sorting into unequal piles presumably distinct, a turning against unimpeded luxuriance? It is like saying we cannot speak as the wind speaks, all caress, all penetration, all uncovering.

And like the Greek tragedian who, each day, lying with the others in an orderly row, gradually raises his voice to the highest treble, who, after playing his rehearsed part, slowly

brings his voice back to the lowest bass and "regains control of it," we know everything by its edge, by its limit, by its concomitant means.

III

Tonight, with snow finally unable to cover everything—that patch beneath the Norway spruce, for example—I think the "Greekling" Demosthenes' story is

the story oratory tells. Demosthenes the stutterer, he "unable to pronounce the initial *r*" in *rhetorica,* unable to name his only devotion, his only distinction. As Cicero asks somewhere:

"What is sillier than to talk about talking?" And so Demosthenes took to putting small pebbles into his oratorical mouth, took to marching up and down

the steep pebble-covered hills near Athens, talking pebble talk. Perhaps he knew the fragility of words and was comforted in spitting them, stone-like, into the silences.

It is as if all necessary eloquence could come only of rejection, of a *leaving behind.* And those real pebbles still burn on the path. They, too, mark an edge, a limit,

that spot where Demosthenes, done with the unseemly Paradise of the continuous remarkable world, turned, forgivably, back to town.

Requiem for a Writing

What if all writing lies
In the blue-note syncopations, the slurry
Margins of the experiential,

There where the brainy neurons, novices, bumble
And slide into one another without so much as an excuse
Me and exactly as if they were the ragtag

Members of a marching band
Trying to form the figure of Dizzy
Gillespie, puffy cheeks, heaven-ascending

Horn, a profile, petroglyphic, imprecise, beckoning?
What if ritual mars memory
The way the brass section is heard

Talking up its lineage, blowing a stew of somebody
Else's melancholia, uncertain mosaic of loss,
Love and gusto? Take any slender moment as example:

Try to pinpoint the true between inkling and hubbub,
In the tremendous inexplicable roar.
What is "played" is a bandleader's

Booklet of jazz standards, sweet
Cheat-sheet of phraseologies, musical
Quotes, mutters of welcome: *Blue Salience*

(The book is lifting off the table), *Bent Horn*
Critique (A dictionary is combing
Big words out of its hair),

Imbrications for a Lady
(Goodbye means goodbye in the sweet by-and-by),
Zoetropismus (An elephant in a porkpie hat is eating

My one and only pencil).

Bookish, Clowning

Uh oh. Here come the insects—click
Beetle, praying mantis, Carolina grasshopper, aphid, green bottle
Fly, the fritillaries—great-

Winged and lesser, red admiral, mourning cloak, spring azure . . .
Naming is a remarkable encounter with a history of compulsion, no?
Its gratifications entwine the ineffable, offer up a plangency that
    enrapts us

Only to unravel as balm to the quotidian itch, oh cut it out.
If I note a scruffy wren the size of a mouse
Rustling up the dry coppery leaves

Under a stand of three hundred-year-old sweetgums, I think of
    Mark
Catesby drawing in the Carolinas, I think of the Frankish dynasty
Of Carolingian rulers, of Christopher Wren, of a white church, its
    tiers

Like a wedding cake, of Christopher Marlowe mouthing off drunk
In a tavern, convinced of genius and bored by it, oh, bored by it.
What is nominal is structural, wrapped in the landscape of its use.

Every word a deposit, a buzzing atomic lode
Of energies, a quark-loud charm, a plait of potential
Singing unheard-of

Songs of radiance and dismay, riffing the umpteen congeries of . . .
Oh the word like any royal behoover needles the clownish to get
    out
One more slaphappy collection of monkeys in a barrel, interlocking,
    toy.

So I spend my days in the company of monkeys, angels
Who perch so capably in droves in the sun-
Blasted heights of trees I know the names of—blue spruce, box

Elder, red
Maple, tamarack, mulberry, oak.
And naming I make an ordinary universe out of a punch line
    behind

Which is no identifiable joke.

The Constabulary

Call to order and I can hardly bring myself
To bring up anything beyond what is absent, meaning just
about everything.
It's as if a *Scenes from the Life of Reilly*
Blocked out on a storyboard consisting of a series of
Empty boxes made a blockade, a checkpoint

Where uniforms of men, blue, prowl like men
Beneath sunglasses that give back no reflections,
Daunting blanks, the taunts and insults
All the more suspect for being unaccompanied by the usual
Growled out pejoratives, grunts and disclosures.

A single word here could open up the situation, turn
Attention away while turning it to
The no landscape of the highway's shoulder
Cut by that sweep of red light rhythmic and tumbling as a
turnstile
Or a lock. Language fails

And not even it can admit it is so.
Undetachable witness to a system it itself
Logs daily, buttering some morning toast, patting pockets for
the key
To the ignition, unable now to step back and say "Officer,
There's been a mistake" without taking a part, its part in the
pantomime.

Dusty Begonias

I used to . . . And the pencil point breaks,
An odd technological failure right here in my fist-
Colored fist. Why honestly lament so if language is just

Like a feather-duster stowed in a back closet,
The one the servants used
To use back in the days . . . And here we go

Snipping the dead blossoms again.
They look like the tiny curls of an homunculus's
Random passions, flailings

Caught in an instant in a grand apartment
With surprisingly rumpled linens on
Beds we remember so clearly . . .

*

We would voyage indefatigably, parting
Streets, lifting the ornery grid up
With a cry against order,

Wanting to comb the landscape flat or
Tease it up into a beehive do, something
With the substance of cotton candy and the sweet

Interlace of mystery.
We would go to the dangerous boathouse and see
Gloom reflecting up like an eye when we bent to put

An eye to a knothole there in the floor's flooring.
We would do whatever the umpteen days arranged
As condiments on a salver offered . . .

*

And I wrote it all down, a pencil
In beach togs and zoris,
A big hand manhandling the moment's symmetries,

In cahoots with the blessèd partiality of
That moment. None of it exists, none of it ever did:
The rapture in the denying I is all,

Knowing
You cannot take a rag to a flower or dust
One with anything, though of course you do.

Perfect Sentences

The snapdragons standing on the settee go
A little droopy in the heat.
Close up, one pale one is mumbling,

An old feller crabbing about the useless
Dentures he keeps in a glass of Alka-Seltzer
Beside the plate that is holding dinner.

Looks as if it is gumming spaetzle,
And bratwurst, looks vaguely German that flower,
And unlaundered, one of the privileges of age.

This is a fiction, and murderous.
This is not so. Beside the flowers
A book of perfect sentences lies open,

One more campaign for order
There where the world is ending.
And if I remove my one good eye, position it

In a circle made by thumb and index finger,
Steady against the page
Like a magnifying glass,

I insist that all the disorder and odor of
The world is there, trapped
Between two words—*genuine* and *bluster*—

In a sentence that reads *All the murderers sentenced*
That day spoke with a kind of genuine bluster of good intentions
That flowered only in the sad gap between cradle and grave.

Sad flowers. Perfect flowers. Flowers thriving like flowers.
I insist the wreckage of the world is elsewhere, not here.
And all sentences are perfect, my murderers.

Herb and Violet

Two characters and only one represents anything
The way a *Bildungsroman* gets built
Like a boat in a cellar with all the attendant anxieties

About getting it out the door, up
The stairs, down the twisty path to the beach.
A dire little exercise in spatial relationships, it

Causes time to drop away, though
Reading back over it you notice time is built
Into the mere grammar or is there hugging the path

Where stones mark out beds of lovage and nasturtium,
Coriander and a dwarf lavender common to the higher climes
Of Galicia, in northern Spain.

I'm not feeling much of anything today, I'm not
Feeling *like* much of anything. Not like that blue pebble
In beak of yon grackle, not like that tousle

Of peony that keeps banging itself against the sunlit entrance
To a regular cave, not like that alarming white
Horse standing in for whatever patch of sky I can make out

Up through all the surrounding encumbrances.
I'm not feeling like the purple sage a sage grows
Merely by saying the lines of a long domestic saga

About Herb, about Violet, about the boating accident
That led to such grumpy characterizations only such a tale
Itself can limn and only if you too

Happen to be stuck in a cellar empty of everything but sawdust,
A sign that construction entails reduction,
Leavings you can count on to help any garden grow.

You sweep it all into a pail, feeling
Like you might as well accomplish one little thing today,
And dump it around the herbs, dump it around the violets.

The Upstart Petunia

On the edge of the field
Rusting so magnificently
Adds its red detritus to the sung world of things.

A signal event.
It is a matter for little circumspection really, just
Take a good look around.

An unending musical staff, five
Fine black lines, parallels the horizon in a grand circle,
Hangs above it like a crude fence.

And notes like hooks, like names, ornament that staff.
There is no key signature
Evident so you turn about, rotating through the evidence

Caught in the boundary, singing
To make the bumblebee be, the salsify be, the dragonfly
And the vireo be, the red kerchief

Lazily settling into the meadow's sweet grasses
Like a tiny parachute
Be, the mud puppy, the lady's slipper, the chanterelle be.

You take it all tunefully into yourself
Standing still in the center, greeting the approaching names,
A temporary shelter and an expulsion,

Successive just to keep
The world in constant motion. A grant to say
The sayable is in a pocket that pockets,

Too, the implements of your listening, the ear
Trumpet hearing aid flower, red,
With its motif of hummingbirds

Needling in to sip, or
The tiny machinery and intricate gear-
Teeth of the parabolic disk rising

White as a handkerchief in the breeze, bringing
Such music to us as we approach the music
We find ourselves waving

A greeting much like a goodbye.

The Wag of the Inconsequent

A hullabaloo in the mist is missed
Due to other inner cadences
Only you seem party to. I mean I.

Attentive to the local,
The only thing to mock
Hereabouts in the mock hereabouts is mockery, so

Interruptions occur in the form of outer larks, a dog
Stopping mid-
Stride

To snap a loud fly out of the air.
No nourishment to it, just something to do
To insert a kind of punctuation

Mark
Into the shimmering text of the morning.
If you stumble against the *what*

In the midst of the *how,* processing the plaintive
Vocables into pure noise
Singular, even if only

For no moment's sustenance, they'll atomize the quick
Into diphthong and sequence,
Warring particulars, the great ha-ha-*haw* . . .

Off the jets of unintelligible truths
There's never no one thing like nothing arriving.
You know. You've scoured the sky.

No contrail scratches remain.
And I means I only by dint of this perfect mock-
Up of myself I's got sitting here

Socializing with the twentieth century, its dirt
Outlining the nail of a finger
Wagging emphatic an accusation

And pointing to the likes of words like *you,*
Unlikely though it is in such surroundings
To be you.

Explication de texte

It's about the wild tones ascending
With honk and clatter on the car-
Strummed avenues at the heated close of day . . .

It's about how one of you stood there
Knock-kneed, raving about inconsequentialities,
The refurbishing of a room.

You loved the soon-to-be-
Ordered disorder of it all
As much as you loved anything.

An historic mountain stood in the background,
Figuring in somehow, all tumulus
And talus, a bump on the hard line of horizon.

For one short period you lived up there
In a shack and burned firewood. The need
To say something—anything—caught

In the terrible middle of you.
In the uptake, in the winch, in the draft.
Something about two

Bluebirds nesting in a box out back.
Something about the box tilting crazy
Against the fence post.

One of you had to go
And name those birds—
Eliot, June—and not particularly aptly,

You add to yourself.
It's about those kinds of additions,
The ones needed, the ones not.

Yaupon, Kouros, Fermata

for Michael Parker

It's a niggardly thing to pare away a whole generous landscape
To one single significant piece
Of shrubbery, or

To follow the drubbing of the Greek soccer team
Only through the infinitesimal feints and near collisions of one
Player, expert at the nutmeg,

Scooting the ball with one quick jab
Between the legs of that Romanian there.
Known words map a geography

That is pure, leave no great hummock in the orderly
Blue pasture smelling of grief, of savory,
Of the way we had to finesse a cumbersome youth

So that we could look back on it with muddy affection
For the sustenance its blackouts and losses provide us with now.
Or we could say those words leave no gap

In a congeries of low mountains,
No one way out of that damn little town that keeps us still
By returning to us a memory—

Two raw peanuts in a shell.
And does that shell with its dirt-slaked cross-
Hatching like that of a pistol's grip

Conform to us or we to it?
This is what we consider in the stop-
Time of fiction, mornings

In lawn chairs under a bungalow's gazebo, sunlight
Holding its one long note above.
It is buttery and yellow and means

The world's chores hang elsewhere, in abeyance.
A blank part of the day, unknown to any usual vocabulary,
    where
Affliction scribbles out the slips of its own cure

And the ending is left to the reader's discretion.

A Jack Spicer Notebook

You don't impose your will on the thing coming through . . .
Language isn't anything of itself.

"Vancouver Lectures"

Rainy washout of a Thursday, what is
Coming through: *spikenard, portulaca, hum.*
And the usual muzzy indelibles
                                        seeing returns,
Tired of the impositions of seeing *beyond:*
Coffee cup and yesterday's coffee cup.
Jack Spicer: "Where we are is in a sentence."

———

(And now I recall Pritchard, all loopy,
                                                giggling in Belmont,
There where the neighbors, white and poor,
Made rage a nightly habit, gunning
Souped-up Camaros
Through the bourbon-etched streets,

Thumping one another in the uninhabitable bruise-light
Of ever-
Docile dawn.
                And Pritchard is butchering the Spanish,
Verde que te quiero verde, giggling like a misfit
Angel, one of the unwary,

One of the dead.)

———

Rainy washout of a Thursday,
Whatever is coming through is transgression and collapse,

An unthrowable switch.
The way music begins

Not here or *here,*
Begins in the nowhere grace
That graces the fraying unseen edge of the immediate.

Where music begins is in the *undoing* of the real:
Unrefereed and implacable, a green fissure
Widening ostensible song into song's
Own unheard-of song.

Spicer: "Words turn mysteriously against those who use them."
Bicycles. Clocks.
                    Green bicycles, green clocks.

———

I am talking about the hard polarity of the summons,
The call,
How it musters up against the real,

Goes belly to belly with that blockhead of an ump
And cannot shout him down.
                                        A thing is here or it is not here.
Our vocabulary is *yes.* Our vocabulary is *no.*

Coleridge: "The apprehension of polarity
Is itself the *basic act of the imagination.*"

Think of the American printer Benjamin Day, inventor
Of the Benday dot,
A way of transforming the wild smear of a photographic
    continuum,

(Unrepresentable, unprintable)
Into an orderly field
(Screened)

Of imaginative decisions:
Every dot inked or not. Here, not here. On. Off.

A switch, a translation.
No other necessary vocabulary. Available.

———

Green how much I want you green.
Rain of a Thursday
Fouling up the switch. Incommunicado.

The useless furniture of the room. Coming through:
Unwilling tokens and these
several keepsakes
Fusty with verdigris.
A collage of the ineffable, the marriage of *yes* and *no*.

The old story of what to do
With a sewing machine, an umbrella, a dissecting table.

———

No disclosure but in the disappearance of the self.
Goodbye, Jack. Goodbye, Pritch.

(And I recall a tornado on the road
To Palmyra,
r & b hawking up a dying cough on the radio . . .

The only other noise that
Of tires pulling
A long stuck bandage off the black wound of the road.

Pritchard's angel and my angel gabbing about metaphor,
Gadding about benign, askew.
                                        Two canaries in a mineshaft.
Two lemons in a trunk.
                                  We were *lit* back then.)

A Notebook of First Permission

a given property of the mind
that certain bounds hold against chaos,

that is a place of first permission,
everlasting omen of what is.
—Robert Duncan

Unenviable weather, long rain breaking
The sweet interstices,
the hidden geometries of snow
Against snow. What weather does

Weather undoes, approximating man. Think of Tristan
Tzara in Paris writing
"to dissolve the hard cement
Of an apparently impregnable fortress: syntax."

———

Out, yards off, a nuthatch, ungroomed, needling
The suet.
Enviable, needling.
Flits off to tree-
Trunk, marks, upside-down, a brief comma.
Slate-blue against the bark.
I am happy enough
Making these few things
Into one thing,
A countenance,

A figure to figure the day against.

———

A sort (a chance throw) of energies:
Uncommon works making savvy the commonality of source,
That big disintegration,
                                        smeary ruthless unboundedness.

One sort (Webster's) is "a piece of type,
A character
Not part of a regular font."

                                              Six years a printer,
The thumping maw of the Chandler & Price,
Handfeeding
                    blank sheets of paper in,
                    words out.

"When all the types in a box are used,
The box is *out of sorts.*"
                                        Printer's terms: *river of white,*
Pigeonhole, staircase, dingbat, quoin, font.

Font: foundry. Foundry: pouring
                                                    a chaos of unsortable liquid
Metal into matrices, making many of one.

A noticeable absence in Paris:
                                                long lambencies of light
Playing over the American field.

The way it brushed up the timothy grasses,
The mullein spears, old
                                        stalks of yarrow and Queen Anne's lace—
A static charge, the "lit within."

What memory does undone by the grammatical what.

That "place of first permission"

Where desire augurs form
And form, unbridled
                                        courses the field of its own making.

The there, where, just

Horsing around becomes the horse.

———

No nuthatch now.

No nuthatch now is a time signature,
A hieroglyph,
A blow of hammer to chisel glancing off

The rock of the page.
                                        No nuthatch now.

Two squirrels, upright
Kettles, two
Question marks, dull ewers, pewter

Vessels with all the inconsequentiality of decorum,

All the consequences of its loss.

Think of Meret Oppenheim taking form where she found it
(Cup and saucer)
And appropriating it
(Lining cup and saucer with fur).

Where form is found is where form founds form.
Tzara: *et tant d'autres et tant d'autres.*

———

Worrying the music, wringing it out:
A desperate alphabet tumbling down the long rain of the sky.
Uncanny proceedings: the way
                                        words go finicky,
Undeliverable, uncountenanced in the unforgettable light.

A need to seize permission, to stop
To unstopper the uncontainable hum.
                                                What works as *frisson*
Is *frisson:* the bell'd tones of Sacré-Coeur
Hanging over the rue Taitbout,
                                        the bronze twitter of the swifts
Unfurling melody as banner.

Down off the little mountain of Montmartre,
Over the white night streets
Of Pigalle,

Over the two lost vineyards
Hunkering, dim, corduroy'd into

Sudden relief in the slanting light . . .

That *place,* unshakable, a syntax.

To Robert Duncan

Sortilege is all, orphan, and *nothing is trivial*—thus by chance machinations, undeflect'd melodies of the unquiet watch, we sound the *What Is,* drifting the boundaried nautical blue,

sentinels to whatever errancy intention—that aimless ward of the imagination—derives of our erring. There we demur, lingering where the western song sparrow's song is unheard of,

where its five struck notes, various, nameable, *some musical, some buzzy,* counsel certainty, a momentary loud sampling, a deft assemblage, welcome awe, and ease.

What's available is the sentence, that *mere story of loving* in the ongoing *decay of intensities,* how it stills the flux of its own leafing out by leaving something out.

This is the law of the *the,* how a simple kind of death inheres in grammar, hermetic, inviolable, new. So we keep moving, we make passages, whole brotherhoods of lost hungers, of

small fires trick'd out of hiding, demure impermanences struck idle and ghostly in the voice-wash, the intercept'd hum of hand-breadth measuring the skittish colt of the page.

We mouth mysteries of music, sere inevitabilities, impure remedies of *pastiche,* yea-saying the lots of irrecoverable Time against that one vacant lot where God is He who imagines Himself.

Sentinel, we keep watch over what we cannot ward off by watching and we make ourselves of nothing and our names of nothing.

Here's a story, orphan: there was a man I never knew who called himself an orphan, a man without a permanent home who in a late recklessness of years wrote a book

that worried the imagination, that, in the reading, seemed to be like taking *pieces of a dissected map out of its box*. He made that up himself. He called truth *a divine ventriloquist.*

In youth, he let the words pour out, mongrel, fecund, dear. He coined equally: *pantisocracy*, *potenziate.* Fearful of *half-knowledge,* that yipping, uncertain,

of dogs in the dark, he declined late into a notably abstract silence. What I mean, sentinel, is this: there is no vanity—that spigot, that spile that draws off sap—

no vanity in *la veille de la vieillesse,* watch of the late watch, no vanity, watcher, in *mere writing,* no vanity in what song is, or what it, song'd, unsings.

Burning Issues

The proliferating ease of the savvy loud theorist is a sign
(In the kingdom of letters)
That the unequivocal upthrust, that particular

Way of pointing to God's contested green
Acreage, is itself contested. Or that's the kind of state
I find myself in, eschewing it

(In a blizzard of modifiers).
So I find an amble through the old neighborhood
A solace, a pummeling need.

Why fistfight with the ordinary?
Quotidian recluses peer out through drawn shades
Where are mapped the byways and hinterlands

Of human need.
Two red-breasted house finches,
Highly musical, prompt

Citizens, return
To a nest they put together in a jiffy one year ago today.
(Needs minor refurbishing.)

(Welcome to the long grasses in the yard.)
Such instinctive teamwork offers
An achingly real pleasure, as does that fiery splinter of
    sunlight

Forcing its way between two houses, reddening
The already red throat of the male.
No more pyrotechnics

Regarding the besieged fealty
Of representation: just two birds, irreducibly there.
And worlds away Gorazde caught in a firefight, igniting

A map of five hundred years of human animosity.
Gorazde, Gorazde, word we repeat
Once as name, contestable, drawn.

Twice as place, irreducible,
Burning, *there,*
Issuing out of a word that's gone.

Rock

Make *rock* contain weight, round solid tonnage or *heft*

And with that an elfin lightness sets in:
Vowel arrangements disturb the molecular,
A density undone.
                    The physical world shredding
Into speech, rocking the nuances of the formable
Histories of things.

                    One rock is resting in an Amagansett field,
A glacially scrubbed chunk of granite, ancient
Keystone to a spring-fed temple unearth'd:

Water unsunned for thirty or so thousand years.

One rock near the Cherwinski farm in northern Michigan
Tops a pile of other rocks
To register the chance articulations
Of a laborer named Roy who left it to last

Over a long August of carrying one by one, emptying out
A corner of the north forty for pasturage,
For beans.
            One rock edges a garden plot
For several seasons of annuals, the yearly sowing
Of tipsy petunias, serious marigolds:

A period unaccountable, a heaven'd blank.

A song is lifting over the antic river.
The rocks are jittery tonight.
                              A man who designs
Useless machines, sketching imaginary transfers of

Useless energies, impure, is gearing up to say a few words.
Rock, he says, *rock* and *rock* and *rock*.

The German Verb "To Twilight"

A solitary black grackle is
Marauding the yard-
Grubs, intent
On nothing and no one but itself, feeding.

Or maybe it's going
Diligently over some stray
Grammatical oddity picked up socially, one
Way of building

A structure
That does not mimic the world so much
As makes it
Bigger, infinitesimally.

The sky
Is a dismal retort to its kind
Of activity, changing
All the time,

Openly insistent.
No simple talk
Of how it lowers its boom of light
Over the Franz Biberkopf Strasse

Will ever be so right as all that
Purity of downfall
And slip to coalesce, what
Trips the unknowable

Integers of an immeasurable thing,
No coefficient,
No shredding,
No parcel.

Hazy Days

Friends, my words are mere consorts
To a dream of unity, heart-
Stopping, gap-ridden scrawls of pure desire,

Landlubbers who, unsteady, having not got sea-
Legs, pursue what cannot be stated
With any assurance, finicky, athwart.

They are like the ghosts of old reruns slipping in
In staticky enforced silence
Into the in-between of channels on a dusty Zenith

And this is no way to explain my distance,
Is not what made it necessary.
All those Christ-in-a-bottle drinks

Never, my God, brought me any nearer to *thee.*
Truth is, I was far, far away all that time—
Gesticulating like an ape seeking the lobotomy

Of heaven, a place we imagine as carved out
Of the hard world like a cave
Carved out of a piece of soap, a place

To allow us to behave, or bereave.
I cannot put it down any better.
Some nights through tears in the polyethylene

Hammered over the windows of that apartment,
I would listen to bird-
Chirp and -mutter, two jays lodging

Youngsters in a loblolly inches away.
The world grew up outside that house.
And I knew that *that* would remain

When I was gone, not representing anything
Beyond itself, not a jot.
Other nights I would shout, wicked with Beefeaters,

About Hart Crane, or,
In a clear isolate place, I would be turning words
In a lottery tumbler: *jodhpur, harmattan, chigger, skiff.*

A tight drum of words, glittery, ex-
Changeable. Fragments inapplicable as these words are
To the story of those days.

And if I say unreasonable things to you now and again
And conjure up makeshift desires dedicated to you
Whom I have lost, it is because the world

Is no fragment, no soap chip,
And with these words I am sudsing up a speculation and a
return.
We could clabber something together together—

For I am a fragment, too.

Mon nom est personne

Big idiocy in outer weather, cur
Heed dogging nobody: there's a simple thought.
Or else one is caught out wearing a standard
        Sundial hat, just

Another sloppy drunk hooting in the dusk.
Winter does funny stuff, mustering its ice-
Soldiers to tap longingly at windows, all
        Bayonets and blue

Reverie, all see-through straight into loud lit
Little cochineal hearts! There's so much going
Down with insects we know so little about:
        One beetle's scutate

Clypeus is rather coccygeal in
Appearance, another's cupped to carry drams
Of God-knows-what buggy cobbler, mint-garnished.
        The vexatious blue

Long about dawn did in a brusque wind cock back
A fist to get the drop on know-how's leavings,
Leavings it'd as lief left for the insects,
        Drunks and leafcutters.

Night and Day in New York

What comes galloping in on the night's sharp hooves comes fully
titled.
What it is called is "A Late Afternoon Trance at the Villa Sober."

It concerns a man purposefully rifling through a great number
of fleet memories.
They seem "machine-generated," quite marvelous in the slow
bloom

Of feverish recuperation. Then, quickly, gone. So he turns
attention to the near
Tender green tomato plants and darker basil sprouting in flats
on the porch,

Where percussive bombardments of sleep molecules shag the
pleasant air
And abstract things written in the margins of *The Book of
Leisure*

Try to set the record straight. Things occurring in the kingdom
are too numerous,
Too devout, and mostly unrecountable, so we invent new
inventories, acceptable

Lacunas in "sense" in order to baffle the bright day. "And I do,
I do
Feel pretty good about that, about my one excursion last week,
the one

To the boat show. It left me with plenty of brochures, flyers
I could send you if you're at all the least bit interested. . . ."
Of course I am.

One afternoon I looked hard and long into the distance and saw
    it move
Closer. There it "stood." Not a foot away. Like an angel in the
    taut light of four o'clock.

And I thought how I could die never having told you:
All those billions of drinks we made off with in our millenarian
    days

Make the present rich with longing for everything I left back
    there,
And the night, when it comes, comes charging like a horse,
    riderless.

Earnest

The staging area is windswept today.

So all the conventioneers see fit to idle the hours away
Leafing through periodicals nobody ever reads
Cover to cover, insanely
Jealous of the tarpaulin haulers

Who are being thrown about like clothespins, spinning

Off the edges of the largesse
That made them take such a job in the first place.
Or so they say.
Everybody knows some event is about to occur.
The camcorders slung like bazookas over the shoulders of

Men with ponytails tell that much.

One night in Soho I saw a man fire a rocket into the air.
Attached to the rocket: a length of rope.
Attached to the rope: the man's Peter Lorre fedora.
A gas from the word go, culminating in the way

That man's hair stuck out every which way like a maestro's

As the hat, beheaded, headed heedless into hatless heights.
I'm trying to be serious about this.
Nothing up my sleeve.
The shirt, though, is one of those Balso Snell models.
I am comfortable in it and so can breezily agree

To disagree about the effects of the wind,

Dropping a little just now.
Maybe we'll be able to do the show after all.
I'd shake on it but I'm afraid
Such an earnest might make

My whole arm come off in your hand.

The Fort and Fortress of Our Certainty

Objects of scrutiny—
A red jersey missing a sleeve,
Torn music, a crow in the rain.
The third heat of the hundred-
Yard dash. Mostly we slouch against door-
Jambs with thumbs hooking
Belt loops, chewing fat, officiating.
To the barricades is what one of a number
Of ants keeps proposing, itching
The back of its shiny black pate
With one threadlike paw
Like a contortionist, like the agent
Provocateur of the untrustworthy grin it is.
Agitprop millions, these black marks
Ticked off in boxes against the checklist of
Our desires. More than one world
Is more than we can take, took
As we are by a serious indebtedness
To the distinct coinages of
Invention, one sentence dogging the heels of another,
Sentient, yes, sentient. Say you ache
To say two things: *bow wow wow* and *Spotty,*
An arrangement out of a book, a dog
You never had. Say its bark
Mutters like a pungent odor, wet
Geraniums craning up graceful and red
Out near the bullpen, an odd place to plant
Such flowers! Everything drops into
Place in a sequence, the starting
Pistol mistook for a call
To arms, spiky penmanship like ant
Tracks recording the stingy transliterations of
A welter of music and grammar
Lashes us blind.

Expiring at the Edge of the Old Empire

O gimme a decent-sized cairn, a bonfire
Built of metaphor's feeble transgressions

Against time's immovable grammar . . .
It did put some of us somewhere though,

Though attention returned to world us, wounding.
Chance is myself is how Artaud put it, hazarding

Recovery, inklings of agency caught in a dialectic, pure
Copula, tautology of muck, pushing out the edges

Of that envelope settling quick into the black
Quicksand where selflessness accounts

For nothing if the world empties itself of the parcels
Of its own delivery . . . We would like to, too,

Clear this matter up before proceeding any further.
We would like to name without renaming—

Book pursuant to book pursuant to boo . . . Fearful stuff.
Truth is, truth resides beside itself, skitters off

Salient as a crayfish, backwards, eyeing
The place it just left like a pointer, ungraspable.

We learn a new language every minute.
We pick up little pointers here and there and dangle

Them like trophies. They are something like ourselves,
Pincers waving wildly, snapping in the empty air.

The Bones in El Bahnasa

In Franklin Delano Roosevelt's stamp collection, there is one specimen picturing the ruins of El Bahnasa, the archaeological dig north of Minya. It's an Egyptian stamp, one of many in Roosevelt's collection, that stamp collection begun at the acquisitive age of seven.

In El Bahnasa today, nobody thinks about F.D.R. It's a sleepy outpost town. On-the-run criminals of various sorts and safari-hatted archaeologists stamp through occasionally. The locals have a phrase meaning *to roll the bones* they use to describe the doings of the archaeologists.

A local poet inhabits the environs, though he is not "much" of a poet. I put the word *much* in quotation marks (though not *poet*) because I am "putting into question" the meaning of *much* in relation to *poet. Putting into question* is also in quotation marks. Just as the word *mug* could be so put.

One cannot drink the somewhat greenish water of the Minya oasis out of a "mug," though out of a mug it can be done. The putting of words into quotation marks is a way *to roll the bones* of the archaeology that is language. What a poet does is a kind of digging to jimmy out the traces of a word.

In *El Bahnasa,* no doubt, there are such traces. Arabic sediments, like the cancellations on a stamp affixed to a letter addressed to Franklin Delano Roosevelt and marked and remarked by every post office on the run between El Bahnasa and the White House. A different poet wrote that letter to F.D.R. fifty years ago.

He mailed it in El Bahnasa. He signed it Ezra Pound though he was not Ezra Pound. *To roll the bones* also refers to a gambler's game played with two dice. It's not unlike *shooting craps.* The roll of the bones the poet took was twofold. One, that the poet's proper identity would not be jimmied out—

that the poet's mug shot would not be found to resemble Ezra Pound's when Ezra Pound, not exactly on the run, stuck in the punishment stockade at the Disciplinary Training Center in Pisa, Italy, mugged for the camera. Two, that the El Bahnasa P.O. would not let the poet's letter slip

down behind the wooden cabinet with its innumerable drawers for stamps. Neither did occur. We can picture, rather, the mug of F.D.R., its rictus grin tilting its overly elegant cigarette holder ever upward, as if *he* were on the run, fearing every next letter to be another rant of some crackpot in Italy.

El Bahnasa he reads through the inky cancellation smudge and neatly cuts, poet or no poet, a stamp-sized squarish bite out of the envelope with a penknife. A mug of coffee goes tepid next to him, undrinkable. He does not read the letter of the poet who signs himself Ezra Pound and lives, he says, near the ruins

of El Bahnasa, also known as Oxyrhynchus. F.D.R. does not think "much" of poets. There is no way to trace a stamp's history—it is like any currency, the stamp. The easiest thing is to roll the bones and gamble that *any* mug on the run, like any word or story, jimmied out or ditched, is, for the moment, the one sought mug.

Depths and Approaches

It's all going by in the air—kitchen
Implements and musical instruments
And duct-taped-up jobbies whose identification is uncertain,
    hence
The particular attention paid out to these latter

As if attention itself were a kind of prior filament
Not readily visible except at the spot where it disappears
Slowly into the all, the way a fisherman's cast-out line sinks
    into black
Depths and approaches the rowboat, indicating less

Where it is than where we are, fishing. "Natural" things go by
    too—welcome
Spirea and peony and jackrabbit and events like the osprey
Raking a smallmouth bass up out of the fog-botched
    reservoir . . .
It's an endless stream, a movie

And is projected once only for the benefit of sailors
Like ourselves, the ones on shore leave who have little else to do,
A weekend to kill, drifting in
For a few hours of what passes

For entertainment in this lousy port,
Aimlessly ratcheting down
Our overly excitable nerves between last mess call and lights
    out, trying
To see the show for what it is

And not muddy it all up with our own . . .
Ours is a somewhat—notice the laconic understatement—
Shorter version and appears to have a structure, some order
To its potshots, its "kitchen sequences," its hellish angles.

Though after a half-day out of the hot Neapolitan sunlight,
Seated and letting our minds do the work while our bodies
    recover,
We begin to suspect something's fishy,
That a bland logical hiatus—something repeatable

As code—is built into the system,
Is a part and parcel of a compartment
Like no other terrifying language and is
What determines now our jittery and eager-

To-get-the-hell-out-of-here comportment.

Order and Accident

Coffee in a cup with a square blue Morris—
Apparently a kind of automobile—
And *Jerry* writ beneath in vaguely Gothic type,

Sunday morning in the first real clemency of weather
And all its ready light, its concussive jazz.
And other words, sentries
Of the gone real, dapple the immediate surround—*aberration,*
Giuseppe, weekly—calling unfinal attention
To worlds and collisions elsewhere, signaling

The unearthly hum of our constant naming and naming of naming.

Just as images do—those tapestry-mimicking
Red doves, say, in a posture of near-
Copulation amongst the roses and dogwoods

Of the sofa's covering, or the open cheer of a book on the cover
Of a closed book, that one dropped nonchalantly
On the coffee table.
I am trying to demarcate
A remarkable plethora of small sensory upheavals, trying
To enter a continuum imperiled
By the discreet

Mediations of the ordinary word
With its square blue contours of desire . . .
The two-year-old Rosa next
door—
Who can now pronounce *wheel, rock, seashell,* who points
With an obvious sense of belonging to the things she arranges

In an order suggesting she is *not* wheel, *not* rock, etc.—is
Just now being reprimanded and lets loose

A long howl of notice that some things remain unarrangeable
Except by howling. It is an accidental distinction she is making:
    how
Naming—*coffee, Sunday*—refuses to still

The ongoing indistinct mergers, the scat of objects

Or the way an elbow in determined trajectory behind a cigarette-
Holding hand will graze a particular Morris cup
And knock it and its coffee all
General and all over
The indistinguishable floor.

Poem Like a Tree or a Bus

Here in the disgathering of general attention,
The citified toots and tweets of the day

With its own collection of jittery particulars, one leaf
Flopping lazily over to get a little sun there

Just to even out its tan. A bus moves off
In a cloud of exhaust

Blotting out two or three bystanders, one
Still fishing in pockets for a token or change that is "correct,"

Indication that the measurable indices change in an inconstant
    way,
Though the coinage does generally seem to keep apace, minting,

And all things seem spendable anew with each spending.
Today I think I am in love with *this* object's desiring

To be plunked down as accommodation
For you and your tendency to look beyond: up the street

To where some other voyagers stand with purpose
Making a series of disconnected thought-

Lines stand out like ridges,
Like tree bark on their brows.

So I put on my most proper day wear, the dark
Pants and white shirt I jimmy open the doors of nit-

Picking propinquity in—
Or with—

And I bring a tie down
Off a hanger casual as any ambassador to a state

Of siege and knot it around the stalk of my neck like a noose.
Let me climb up on that old yellow bus there.

Let me swing down off the only dead
"Limb" "remaining" "on" "that" "tree."

John Latta, in a Copybook

And Georges Seurat, bustling about under the eaves . . .
He's busy turning a number of lines, a
Sketch, something put down in a mannish hurry

After a swim in a black wool *maillot,*
Into a done thing, a thing done with
Points of paint, hundreds and hundreds of discrete

Particulars, like words. It is one way of
Making the world notice that the picture is
Not the world, and that the nomenclature of

Ruthless smeary wash and shadow adjustment imposes a
Queer stability on all the worldly mayhem. Shill
Recovery of the irrecoverable. Torque and suspense of

The sleight-of-hand master. One blue Sunday
I am again walking the continual miles out
To that island in the Seine I first took

Note of in Chicago, humming my deeds like
A cowboy in a slaughterhouse. *Isle de la*
Grande Jatte, solid rip, gape of dirty mouth,

Junkyard of syllables, eater of the dead—a
Place of angels gone to bragging, walking rosy-
Antenna'd giant crustaceans on ropes. I am looking

In every cave and under every tangly green
Droop of willow for Alfred Jarry—I got a number of
tricks with a lariat I think he'd appreciate.

I am looking for Seurat's monkey, I keep
Hearing its vatic bark, its rictus doubter's mirth.
Because they say that in the loud inventories

Of a copybook, hubbub itself is one centrality.
Because it shouts the name of its appraisals,
Because it overlays its colors pure in order

To make the canvas the palette. I write
It all down in a little copybook:
"A reminder—the two words buried in *remainder."*

Marketable

Staunchly bullish the proddings in the durable
Goods department where an excess of
Sundries continues in proper array, encyclopedic
Like the dispersion of stationery items, paper

Clips and whatnot, secure in the cubby holes
Of my infamous rolltop desk, that stronghold. . . .
The report may begin like that, courteous
And eager as a man folding the trousers

He has just slipped out of,
Or knotting the swim trunks
He has just slipped into, the blue chlorine-
Spiked pool racing out its swim

Lanes right there in front of him.
He isn't sure he ever *was* a child, never
Here, in this land of memos and mouthwashes,
And the bouncy idiocies of big sex

Briefs filed on behalf of
Lonely clients, all of them drink-
Primed for the hauntingly predictable repartee.
He is seeking a return to something

He may still recognize by its inadequacy,
Some single fierce truth beyond
The giddy palimpsest of language, beyond
The scumble and hush of word and desire . . .

So anything may begin in this twentieth
Century of contextual consensus, that
Umbrella we keep lording over our self-
Consciousnesses, standing poolside in our tiny trunks.

Exclusive

The neighborhood isn't "up"
Or is so before me and is gone
Off to toilsome adventures elsewhere,
What is called the quotidian,
A kind of daily smarting
Where pricks of accomplishment out-
Run desire and so leave a trace
Of mutual disaffection made light of only
By backslapping odd familiarities
And the denatured commodities of
Grin and sympathy, gin and the ersatz
Tonic, a grand production, a progress . . .
Enough to make anyone a homebody.
So I run through streets of empty houses
And am dogged by dogs,
Simple, vociferous, exact.

I would rather say: beyond the beyond
A purse hangs like a bracelet off
The wrist of an angel. I would rather admit
That it is full of currency,
Unapproachable, unnamed, unmanned.
In one myth a goodly portion of baggage
Is lost by a shepherd, an illiterate
Greek, all curls and stammer,
And its lack is what one is supposed
To cherish, Dogberry to an absolute.
I say: this is mischief and you too
Will come to grief, my miscreant.
I say, too, that the sun descends
So blazingly on my two feet it lights "up"
My two socks—sun like sun, socks like socks,
Simply marvelous to relate—

A real *mirabile dictu* running through
The neighborhood like an everlasting no.

Wisdom Terrestrial and Nigh

Hurrah for us wiseacres, us
Earthlings who pout in the glamorous soup
Of airs we never put on with any success, democratic

As trees though.
Thorough our thought is though
Not exactly filling, our maneuvers those of mules

Hugging the sure contours of the map's bumps
And bridges, anything that divides land
Up into the here and there.

There deaf fathers of our country
Count out into pockets empty of everything mere
Tobacco curls, pine

Shavings, little tortures of lint and vermilion.
And here we in I's guise
Long to welcome you

Into the impartial embrace of a desire to number
Beyond the imprecise
Many.

Long to disturb the angelic mummery of unrinsed perpetual
    night
All soapy with stars through sheer strength
Of love, its inchoate prowess

Like that of a bee,
Its stinger dropping off, imbedding under skin like an itch to
    recover
A meaning

That will not save us and will not let us continue to be damned
Though the instruction manuals
Say opposite

In acres of print, in words that lie
On the page in rows and furrows and send out rootlets, tendril-
Fine, and tubers that knot up

Rhizomic, a net
Labyrinthine where glossary is only appendage
Though firm we stand, and cross, and fertile, and on indubitable
earth.

Glib

And then late one evening a conversation
In the blue peppery light of dusk
Makes a dilatory moment big
As sure serenity attaches itself to a terror
Of happiness and happiness is
Possibility, that yellow history
Of would have been and will not be, all of it

Cupped in the slender ivory boat
Of the quiet rising moon.
As we cease our talking, my fingers pause
To write out a clumsy alphabet,
An ongoing perfect syntax of blood,
Vessels, blue sentences under the skin
Of a wrist, your own.

I go the route of the bashful student, undone
Into speech by the implications of one final thing,
What I thought I needed not point out
About that Chekhov story:
Gurov only sees what he is by seeing Anna as Anna.
Maybe the world is truly indifferent
To our own noticings, that botch

Of self signaling wildly to self.
Certainly the nightshade's dark berries are—
Hanging in plump clusters over the storm fence—
With us in this brute cohesion.
Untended, they come up thick,
Roping themselves round the woodpile.
In the planet's sly gravity they are heavy enough

To be in reach of the two-year-old Rosa
Who's lately been asking her mother if she can eat them.
Tomorrow we'll take the pruning shears out
And make destruction one of our chores.
Those nightshade vines'll come back and Rosa's attention
By then will be turned to other, less plain, mysteries.
I don't want to talk anymore now though.

The sleek skiff of the moon is sailing through the cloudless
night
And you are here stirring a little, suppressing
A yawn and letting it go in the ease
No talk allows. That moon is overloaded
And terror is at the oars, pulling breathlessly its long strokes,
Joyful, intermittent, and wed
To this moment and all of what happiness contains.

Unfinished

Stereopticon, diminuendo, triplet—all
Very *à la mode* right now
In the shivery void of fleeting years . . .

All the turgid hesitancies of music
Augmenting the mystery of
That page that is written *down* . . .

Language, like water, seeks a level of its own,
Never deep enough to swim in, though bottomless,
Enough to get you wet.

Just so, you love the breezy certitude
Of the listing millions, the stalks of humankind
Who frequent the dictionaries, maintaining

An inhuman kind of order
In the ordinary arbitrations of the arbitrary—
Reckless, alphabetic, fun.

———

What is unfinished sketches in
Blasts of heartache, tropes of desire,
Places wherein reside both wonder and regret, like *here*

Where a simple pencil mark divvies up
A breast into nipple, pout and plenitude,
Or draws you down into the damp

V-suggestion of an ordinary vagina.
In infinitesimal hazard you scrimp
To make reduction itself a destiny,

The only bookable act in town.
Wrong. Slide any card, dog-eared and sepia,
A duotone print of Old Faithful's cooked water blowing sky-
high,

Into the Viewmaster's slot and trust
Whatever you make out is unavoidable synthesis—
Pleasant, breezy, wet.

Look

Seeing is a concern
Radical enough in its usual unconcern
To untether itself, to unhitch the seen

And trot it off unnoticed, *as* the unnoticed,
Though I do see now how the unclipped grass
Across the street is a green mob of greens.

The sun is hitting it
And a lazy skiff of wind is riffling
The individual blades—like a whole uprooted tribe

Amassed and brandishing
Spears of white light.
(That's not seeing.) (That's not grass.)

Ordinary scrutiny of the ordinary grass: what's extraordinary
Is how green is a caution . . .
It is the color of ambivalence, it is the color of angelic
    necessity . . .

Green sunlight and breeze.
Something invisible as thought
Is pawing the pointy thoughtless

Sequins of a semiformal gown, green and variegated,
A sleek shimmer, recumbence on a lawn.
(That's not it.)

So go the idiot riffs of a mad combo—
Every single squeezed-out note
A music *and* a metaphor

You always accept without knowing it.
All the otherworldly spectacles of green—Zulu uprising,
Post-cocktail *déshabillé*—and green itself escapes in the garment

Of your looking,
Falls like music into the perfect daily order
Of the inexpressible, unseen.

A Template, Receding

What we measure the clamorous slapdash present with,
Holding it up so as to mitigate its uncertain roaring.
The eye and the hand in tandem

Collapse the bounty of the marina, all that grind and slap
Of rigging, the furtive barnacles wildly pumping
The water below the waterline, robbing it of nutrient, of diatom.

Focus is always a kind of lie so we move away and go sketchy:
A row of white and haphazard triangular shapes, tilting in blue.
The sound is not silent either. It prickles and hums, near

Endlessly, mocking our heart's cache of tracks, musical
Or industrial, collected and laid down by busy sound
Engineers for radio stations mostly, one in Geneva, Switzerland,

One in Helena, Montana. Tracks laid down by the heart's attempt
To contain the mutable splash, the ongoing shift and recovery
Of water making watery noises with water,

A feckless spooling out and rewind, a standard dance down below
The other, slower dance going on up against the horizon.
We are too far away now to make out anything beyond

The merest specks of light. They are blinking
Like language blinks, now on, now off
Where the present is no longer,

Where the indices of change
Change and you have to start making it all up or leaving
Its finish, like the world's, unfinished.

John Latta

is the author of *Rubbing Torsos,* and the recipient of numerous awards, including two NEA creative writing fellowships. His poems have appeared in a wide variety of publications including *Boston Review, New American Writing,* the *Gettysburg Review, Jacket,* and *Chicago Review.* Latta received his A.B. in English from Cornell University, where he founded the literary magazine *Chiaroscuro.* He earned an M.F.A. in Creative Writing at the University of Virginia and a Ph.D. in English at the State University of New York, Albany. Latta works at the University of Michigan's Harlan Hatcher Graduate Library.

www.ingramcontent.com/pod-product-compliance
Lightning Source LLC
LaVergne TN
LVHW020637100826
845148LV00012B/2217

* 9 7 8 0 2 6 8 0 2 1 7 1 9 *